Tiger

Macdonald

About Macdonald Starters

Macdonald Starters are vocabulary controlled information books for young children. More than ninety per cent of the words in the text will be in the reading vocabulary of the vast majority of young readers. Word and sentence length have also been carefully controlled.

Key new words associated with the topic of each book are repeated with picture explanations in the Starters dictionary at the end. The dictionary can also be used as an index for teaching children to look things up.

Teachers and experts have been consulted on the content and accuracy of the books.

A MACDONALD BOOK

© Macdonald & Co (Publishers) Ltd 1971

First published in
Great Britain in 1971

This edition first published in
Great Britain in 1986

British Library Cataloguing in Publication Data
Tiger. – (Starters)
    1. Readers – 1950 –
    I. Title
    428.6   PE1119
      ISBN 0-356-03547-6
      ISBN 0-356-11490-2 Pbk

Printed and bound in Great Britain by
Purnell & Sons (Book Production) Ltd,
Paulton, Bristol

Published by Macdonald & Co (Publishers) Ltd
Maxwell House
74 Worship Street
London EC2A 2EN

Members of BPCC plc

Illustrator: Isobel Beard

Here is a baby tiger.
A baby tiger is called a cub.
This cub lives in India.

1

The mother tiger carries the cub
in her mouth.
The mother tiger is a she-tiger.
A she-tiger is called a tigress.

2

The cub has a brother and sister.
The cubs are two days old.
They take milk from their mother.

3

After six weeks the cubs can drink water.
Their mother takes them to the water hole.

Sometimes the sun is very hot.
The cubs keep cool in the long grass.

5

Tigers eat other animals.
The mother tiger kills animals for the cubs.
6

The mother tiger shows the cubs
how to hunt.

Now the tiger is three years old.
He is almost fully grown.
He can hunt by himself.
He hunts at night.

8

The tiger is hungry.
He can smell the wild pigs,
but he cannot see them.

He comes close to the pigs.
His stripes help to hide him.
10

Suddenly the wind changes.
Some of the pigs smell the tiger.
They start to run away.

The tiger rushes out.
He can run very fast for a short time.
12

The tiger pounces on one of the pigs.
He can leap a long way.

Now it is day.
The sun is very hot.
The tiger sleeps under a tree.
14

The tiger can swim very well.
He swims in the river.
The water keeps him cool.

Sometimes the tiger catches fish.
Sometimes he catches crocodiles too.
16

One day the tiger meets a tigress.
He wants her as his mate.

He keeps other tigers from his tigress.
18

Soon the tigress has her cubs.
They are born in a den.
The tigress licks their fur.

Long ago there were many tigers.
Some people killed tigers with spears.
20

Many tigers have been shot with guns.
Today there are not so many tigers.
We must take care of them now.

cheetah

leopard

lion

jaguar

lynx

bobcat

See for yourself

Look for the tiger in the zoo.

The tiger is one of the cat family.

These animals are in the cat family too.

Look for them at the zoo.

Starter's **Tiger** words

cub
(page 1)

grass
(page 5)

India
(page 1)

hunt
(page 7)

tigress
(page 2)

wild pig
(page 9)

water hole
(page 4)

stripes
(page 10)

23

pounce
(page 13)

den
(page 19)

fish
(page 16)

lick
(page 19)

crocodile
(page 16)

spear
(page 20)

mate
(page 17)

gun
(page 21)